A Robbie Reader

Meet Our New Student From

COLOMBIA

Rebecca Thatcher Murcia

Mitchell Lane
PUBLISHERS

P.O. Box 196
Hockessin, Delaware 19707
Visit us on the web: www.mitchelllane.com
Comments? email us: mitchelllane@mitchelllane.com

Mitchell Lane
PUBLISHERS

Meet Our New Student From

Australia • China • **Colombia** • Great Britain
• Haiti • Israel • Korea • Malaysia • Mexico
• New Zealand • Nigeria • Tanzania

Copyright © 2009 by Mitchell Lane Publishers

Printing   1   2   3   4   5   6   7   8   9

PUBLISHER'S NOTE: The facts on which the story in this book is based have been thoroughly researched. Documentation of such research can be found on page 45. While every possible effort has been made to ensure accuracy, the publisher will not assume liability for damages caused by inaccuracies in the data, and makes no warranty on the accuracy of the information contained herein.

To reflect current usage, we have chosen to use the secular era designations BCE ("before the common era") and CE ("of the common era") instead of the traditional designations BC ("before Christ") and AD (*anno Domini*, "in the year of the Lord").

Library of Congress Cataloging-in-Publication Data
Murcia, Rebecca Thatcher, 1962–
   Meet our new student from Colombia / by Rebecca Thatcher Murcia.
       p. cm. — (A Robbie reader)
   Includes bibliographical references and index.
   ISBN 978-1-58415-650-5 (library bound)
   1. Colombia—Juvenile literature. I. Title.
   F2258.2.M87 2008
   986.1—dc22
                                                        2008020887

PLB

CONTENTS

The streets of Cartagena, a city on the Colombian coast, are famous for their colonial buildings.

Camila Is Coming!

Chapter

"With liberty and justice for all." Carol Martin finished saying the Pledge of Allegiance with the rest of her class at Jim Thorpe Elementary School in Akron, Pennsylvania. She was excited because it was almost time for winter vacation. Her cousins were coming to visit from Virginia. She hoped it would snow so that they could go sledding.

"Good morning, class!" said Mrs. Johnson, interrupting her thoughts. "I have some exciting news. A new family just moved to our neighborhood from Colombia." She pronounced the country's name as *koh-LOHM-bee-ah*. "One of the girls, Camila Ramos, will be joining our class next week."

The entire class looked at the teacher in surprise. "Colombia! That's far away," said Mario.

Carol raised her hand.

"Yes, Carol?"

The Toco toucan is one of many species of toucans that live in Colombia. Its beak is nearly 10 inches long, and it eats mainly fruit.

"Will she know any English?" Carol asked. "I thought they spoke Spanish in Colombia. And why did you pronounce *Colombia* that way? It sounded funny."

The other students laughed, but they understood Carol's point. They were used to hearing *Colombia* pronounced *kuh-LUM-bee-ah*.

Mrs. Johnson smiled at Carol. "We need to learn more about Colombia before Camila arrives," she said. "But I can tell you that in Spanish, the country's name is pronounced *koh-LOHM-bee-ah*. Camila's first language is Spanish, but she has studied English in school."

"Speaking of her school," Mrs. Johnson continued, "there is something else that might surprise you." She walked over to the big calendar on the wall. First she flipped all the way back to February, at the beginning of the year. "Camila actually started third grade back in February." She pointed to the calendar page, then flipped rapidly forward. "And she just finished at the end of November. So Camila will actually be *back* in third grade with us next week, but since she needs to learn a little more English, and she wants to learn more about being in the United States, it will be fine."

Carol raised her hand quickly and asked: "So she didn't finish the year in June and have a summer vacation like we do here?"

Chapter 1

"Exactly," Mrs. Johnson answered. "Most of the schools in Colombia end the year in November and then have their long vacation over December and January. They also have a short vacation in July, after the first two marking periods."

Mrs. Johnson walked over to the world map and pointed to Colombia. It was at the top of South

Men in Cartagena, Colombia's colorful city on the Caribbean coast, play chess with bottles that are painted and filled with sand. Behind them is a *chiva*, a traditional brightly decorated truck used for bringing peasants and their crops to market.

Coffee is Colombia's most important crop. One reason Colombian coffee is popular is an advertisement based on "Juan Valdez," who is supposed to be a typical Colombian coffee farmer.

America, just below the narrow country of Panama. "We want Camila to feel welcome," she said. "So during the next few days we are going to study the map of Colombia, and the country's history and culture. We are even going to make some Colombian food."

Carol could not wait to learn more about Colombia—or to meet Camila.

Native Colombians try to preserve their traditions and their language.

Colombia's History

Chapter 2

The Chibchas—the native people of what is now Colombia—lived in the rich farmland in the high plains of the center of Colombia. Researchers believe they were living there from 1000 BCE. The Chibchas grew corn, potatoes, and other crops. Unlike the Incas of Peru and the Mayas of Mexico and Central America, they did not build temples or pyramids. They did, however, create beautiful pottery and gold jewelry.

Explorers from Spain arrived in Colombia in 1499. They came just a few years after Christopher Columbus had dared to sail across the Atlantic and found North America. At the time, the royal family of Spain was sending explorers to the New World to look for gold and new lands to conquer. Over the next few hundred years, many of Colombia's native people died from illnesses brought from Spain and other countries in Europe. Others died when they were forced to work as slaves in the gold mines.

CARIBBEAN SEA

Where in the World

Puerto Bolívar

Santa Marta

Barranquilla

Cartagena

Pico Cristóbal
Colón

PANAMA

Turbo

VENEZUELA

Cúcuta

Bucaramanga

Medellín

Pereira

BOGOTÁ

Meta River

Ibagué

PACIFIC OCEAN

Buenaventura

La Mesa

Cali

COLOMBIA

Popayán

Pasto

Mitú

EQUATOR

ECUADOR

AMAZONAS

BRAZIL

PERU

Amazon

Leticia

FACTS ABOUT COLOMBIA

Total area: 439,735 square miles
(1,138,910 square kilometers)

Population: 45,013,674 (July 2008 est.)

Capital City: Bogotá

Religion: Roman Catholicism (90 percent)

Official Language: Spanish

Chief Exports: Petroleum, coffee, coal,
nickel, emeralds, clothing, bananas, cut
flowers

Monetary Unit: Colombian peso

The settlers called the country New Grenada, and it included Colombia, Venezuela, and Panama. The kings and queens of Spain chose Spanish men to govern New Grenada. Their rule was fairly peaceful until about 1776. When the North American colonists defeated the king of England and won their **independence** (in-dee-PEN-dents), people in other parts of the world began fighting against their rulers as well.

Led by Simón Bolívar, a general from Venezuela, the colonists declared independence from Spain on July 20, 1810. When the colonists won the war in 1819, they named Bolívar president.

Although Bolívar was a good general, he was no George Washington. He favored having a dictator—one powerful person—control the government. He also gave the Catholic Church, which had been the main religion in the colony since the beginning, a special role as the new country's official church.

Those who supported the Catholic Church's role formed the Conservative Party. Those who opposed it formed the Liberal Party. The two parties fought, on and off, for the next 150 years.

In 1903, just after the War of a Thousand Days, Panama declared its independence from Colombia. The United States, which wanted to build a **canal** (kah-NAL) across Panama, supported Panama's independence.

The worst period of violence began in 1946 and continued for ten years. During this time, Jorge Eliécer Gaitán of the Liberal Party was running for president. In 1948, he was **assassinated**. Fighting broke out across the country. More than 200,000 people were killed in what became known as La Violencia, or The Violence.

To end the killing, leaders of the two parties formed a **unified** (YOO-nih-fyd) government called National Front. The two parties would take turns electing a president, until 1974, when regular elections were begun again. The National Front stopped La Violencia, but the people were still not happy. A few people were rich and owned large farms, while the poor often had no land and went hungry. Some wanted their government to be **democratic** (deh-moh-KRAH-tik), and others wanted it to be **socialist** (SOH-shuh-list).

fun FACTS

In 1773, the American colonists threw British tea into Boston Harbor to protest King George III's taxes. Colombian colonists also protested the Spanish crown's new taxes. They burned tobacco and dumped alcohol in their own version of the Boston Tea Party in 1781. The revolt eventually led to the Colombian War of Independence.

In the 1960s and 1970s, guerrilla (guh-RIH-luh) armies rose up throughout **Latin America**. Many of the fighters were inspired by the victory of the Cuban **revolutionaries** (reh-vuh-LOO-shuh-nay-rees). In Cuba, the people had overthrown their government and installed a socialist system. The Union of Soviet Socialist Republics (USSR), which included present-day Russia, also wanted to help Colombian guerrilla fighters make their country socialist.

Emigrants from Colombia led marches against the main guerilla army in Colombia, the FARC, in capitals all over the world on February 4, 2008. These protesters gathered in Montevideo, Uruguay.

Manuel Marulanda, whose real name was Pedro Antonio Marín, founded the FARC in 1966. He died of a heart attack in March 2008.

In Colombia, the biggest guerrilla army was known as the FARC, the Spanish initials for the Armed Forces for the Colombian Revolution. The FARC took over huge pieces of land. They gave some of this land to poor Colombian farmers, who had received little help from the Colombian government.

In some countries around Colombia, such as in El Salvador, the guerrillas tried to make peace with their governments. But in Colombia, the FARC grew larger and stronger. To raise money for their cause, they began to produce and ship illegal drugs. They also kidnapped people. By the 1990s, Colombia was a scary place.

Alvaro Uribe, who was elected president in 2002, promised to arrest the drug **traffickers** (TRAA-fih-kers) and to send more soldiers to fight the guerrillas. While some Colombians did not agree with his plan, Uribe made Colombia more peaceful. He was reelected in 2006 and remained popular in 2008.

Colombia

The eastern plains of Colombia lie between the Andes mountains and the border with Brazil.

Colombia's Geography

Chapter 3

Colombia's geography ranges from steamy rain forests bordering the mighty Amazon River to high mountains covered with snow and sandy beaches on a breezy coast. Let's take a quick tour of this amazing country.

In the far south is Leticia, a city along the Amazon River. It is in the Colombian department, or state, known as Amazonas, one of the largest of the country's thirty-two departments. Amazonas is thickly covered with tropical plants and trees, which release oxygen for Earth's atmosphere. That is why the Amazon region is known as the lungs of the earth. The area has high temperatures and frequent rainstorms.

The **endangered** (en-DAYN-jerd) pink river dolphin lives in the Amazon River. It is one of the many types of animals that suffer whenever the rain forest is destroyed. Leticia is the urban center of Colombia's

fun FACTS

Colombia has several popular national parks along its Caribbean coast. One is the Islas Rosarios, or the Rosary Islands, where snorkelers can see many different coral formations and fish. Another is the Tayrona, a park that includes the Nevada Santa Marta, the highest seaside mountain in the world. Near Cartagena, tourists enjoy soaking inside a mud volcano. They say the mud has healing powers.

fun FACTS

Amazon region. The residents of the area—many of them native people—work in rain forest **conservation** (kon-ser-VAY-shun), fishing, and tourism.

In Colombia's northwest, closer to the Pacific coast, are the craggy Andes mountains. This long mountain range begins in Chile at the southern tip of South America and continues all the way through Colombia to Venezuela. The Andes are part of what is known as the Ring of Fire, because many of the mountains are volcanoes.

Farther north along the Andes, the temperature drops, and the mountain range becomes dotted with snowcapped peaks. The historic town of Popayán has colonial churches and other very old brick buildings with matching red roofs. Near Popayán, the mountain range divides into three branches, the western, central,

The Nevado del Ruiz volcano erupted in 1985, killing about 20,000 residents of the nearby village of Armero.

and eastern **cordillera**. Living among these peaks is the huge Andean condor, a graceful bird that is a Colombian national symbol. Its wings, from tip to tip, can span 10 feet!

Between the eastern and the central mountain ranges is the high plain of Bogotá, on which sits the capital city of Bogotá. About 8 million people

The Andean condor ranges from Colombia down through the Andes to Chile. It prefers to feed on large dead mammals, such as cattle or deer.

live in the city. The rich soil surrounding the city is excellent for raising cattle and growing vegetables and other crops. To the east of Bogotá lie the vast eastern plains, which are a little like Texas, with oil wells and cattle ranches. Capybaras (kah-pee-BAYR-uhs) are common in these plains. About as big as a large dog, capybaras are the largest rodent in the world.

fun FACTS

The Nevado del Huila is the highest volcano in Colombia, reaching 17,844 feet above sea level. After staying calm for 400 years, it erupted in 2007 and again in April 2008.

It gets hot again near the Magdalena River, which is similar to the Mississippi River in the United States. The river leads from the land to the west of Bogotá all the way north to Barranquilla on Colombia's Caribbean coast. This coast is famous for its sunny beaches and for the old city of Cartagena (kar-teh-HAY-nuh). The city was made into a fortress for storing gold during the time of the Spanish rule. Every year, many tourists visit Cartagena's huge walls, restored colonial buildings, and museums.

Farther up the coast is the department of La Guajira (lah gwah-HEE-rah), on the **peninsula** (peh-NIN-suh-

The San Felipe castle, which the Spaniards used to defend Cartagena from pirates, towers over the city of Cartagena.

The native Chibcha people of Colombia created ornate crafts from gold. Today Bogotá is host to a popular gold museum where visitors can see examples of the ancient artwork.

luh) between Colombia and Venezuela. Near the border is El Cerrejón (sayr-eh-HON), the biggest open-pit coal mine in the world. There are also mines in Colombia that produce gold, emeralds, and diamonds. How is that for amazing geography?

Colombia

The San Francisco Church is in Popayán, in the south of Colombia. Beautiful Catholic cathedrals adorn the main plazas in towns throughout Colombia.

Life in Colombia

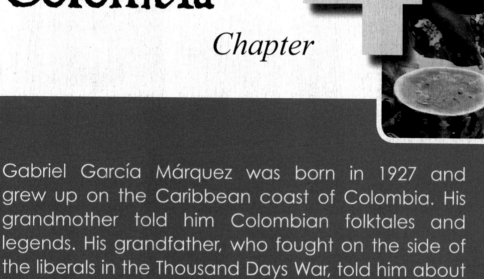

Chapter 4

Gabriel García Márquez was born in 1927 and grew up on the Caribbean coast of Colombia. His grandmother told him Colombian folktales and legends. His grandfather, who fought on the side of the liberals in the Thousand Days War, told him about Colombia's history.

When Gabriel was older, he worked as a newspaper reporter. He started writing novels on the side. *One Hundred Years of Solitude*, which was published in English in 1970, is the richly detailed, magical story of the Buendía family in the imaginary town of Macondo.

The book made García Márquez popular around the world, and for it he won the Nobel Prize for literature. Readers throughout the world felt as though they had come to know Colombian culture from García Márquez's work.

Like the fictional Macondo, Colombia remains a society that is divided between rich and poor. Rich Colombians can go to elegant malls to buy the latest brand-name clothes and shoes. Meanwhile, poor Colombians struggle to feed their children and send them to school.

Colombians tend to be very friendly, yet formal. Children do not address adults by their first names. They use titles such as *señor* (Mr.) or *señora* (Mrs.). When visitors arrive at a Colombian's house, they

Colombia is a wealthy country, but the riches are not shared equally. Many Colombians struggle to feed their children and buy them clothes for school. Poverty in the countryside has been made worse by the war.

These Colombian children have made toys out of plastic bottles. Colombian children also make soccer balls by tying rags together, and they play "kick the can" with a soda bottle filled with dirt.

are offered coffee, soda, or *agua de panela*, a popular kind of tea made from raw sugar. When Colombians visit each other, they almost always bring a small gift, even if it is just a plump, ripe mango.

About 90 percent of the people in Colombia are Roman Catholic. During the year, Colombians celebrate some of the same holidays as Catholics in the United States, such as Christmas and Easter. They also celebrate many holidays based on the

calendar of the Roman Catholic Church. For example, they celebrate Saint Joseph's Day on March 19, and Three King's Day on January 6. Holy Week, the week between Palm Sunday and Easter, is a required vacation from school.

Colombians also celebrate Independence Day (July 20) and many other holidays. They will often eat a special, traditional meal such as tamales, which are made with corn and meat that are wrapped and steamed inside banana leaves.

Colombians are very patriotic. They love their national anthem, which is played on the radio every day at 6:00 P.M., and their flag. In this Independence Day march on July 20, 2003, Colombians carried a flag that was more than a mile long through the streets of Bogotá.

fun FACTS

The New Year is a huge holiday in Colombia. On New Year's Eve, Colombians often sweep the streets and paint the front of their houses to get ready for a big outdoor party. Many Colombians believe that wearing yellow underwear will bring them good luck during the next year. They make a straw man called "The Old Year," which also means "The Old Man" in Spanish, and then explode him with gunpowder at midnight.

Children usually go to school from 8:00 A.M. to 1:00 P.M. They have a snack during the day and then eat lunch when they arrive at home. However, as schools become more and more crowded, some children must go in the afternoon instead, from 1:00 P.M. to 6:00 P.M.

Schools in Colombia have two uniforms. One is a regular uniform, which includes shoes that have to be shined, and slacks or a skirt and a button-down shirt that have to be ironed. The second uniform includes sneakers, sweatpants, and a polo-type shirt that is used for sports and physical education days. Music and dance are an important part of school and life in Colombia. Students often perform dance and musical concerts with costumes.

During cultural week, Colombian schoolchildren dress in costumes and perform plays and concerts. Kindergarteners in La Mesa dressed up as Mexican mariachis.

Soccer is popular in Colombia, as it is throughout Latin America. Colombian national team player Carlos Sanchez dribbles the ball past an Irish player during a friendly game in 2008.

Soccer is Colombia's national sport, but Colombians enjoy many other activities, including riding bicycles up and down the country's many mountains. They have also invented games such as the very popular *tejo* (TAY-hoh), which is sort of like a cross between darts and horseshoes. Players throw heavy metal disks at a target, and if they hit a bull's-eye, little triangles of gunpowder explode.

Camila's cousins and their best friends ham it up on the front porch of their house in La Mesa.

Camila showed us pictures of her older brothers, Gabriel and Mario, on their way to school.

Hola, Camila!

Chapter

5

The week before Camila arrived seemed to pass quickly. The day before she came, the class split into pairs. Each pair received a piece of cardboard and a little bag containing dry corn, dry beans, lentils, coffee beans, and rice.

"In Colombia, people use the seeds they have handy to create pictures and fancy signs," Mrs. Johnson said. "I want each team to decide what to make. You can write *Bienvenido*, which means 'welcome' in Spanish, or you can look at some of these pictures from Colombia and re-create them." She held up a poster showing a farm on a hillside, with coffee and banana plants around it. She also showed the class a picture of a coffee farmer and his mule.

"These coffee beans smell good," Carol said. She and her friend Nick were gluing the beans to cardboard to make a picture of a farmhouse. When they were finished, the class would hang up their pictures to make Camila feel more at home.

The next day, Camila walked into the room with her mother. She was wearing a blue denim skirt, a pink polo shirt, and a red jacket. Her hair was tied back neatly in a ponytail. She looked nervous.

"Hello, Camila," our teacher said, walking over to the new girl. "My name is Mrs. Johnson, and this is your new class. They have something they want to say to you."

"*Hola!*" the whole class said together. "*Bienvenido!*"

We had learned some other Spanish words, too. Mrs. Johnson had written some of them on the board:

Spanish	Pronunciation	English
casa	KAH-sah	house
desayuno	des-EYE-oo-noh	breakfast
gracias	GRAH-see-us	thank you
por favor	por fuh-VOR	please
si	see	yes

A little smile tugged at the corners of Camila's mouth. Mrs. Johnson showed her where to put her coat and backpack, and where to sit.

"We have been studying Colombia all week," Mrs. Johnson said, walking over to a map of the country. "Can you show us where you lived?"

Camila pointed to a small city west of the capital. "La Mesa," she said softly. "We lived in a *casa* that belonged to my grandfather. On Sundays I went to the market with my grandmother."

Camila took this picture of her teachers and classmates at her school in Colombia. Along with the same subjects studied in the United States, such as math and social studies, Colombian children also take classes in religion, ethics, and law.

The students had learned that Colombians eat cheesy arepas (uh-REE-puhs), which are thick tortillas made from cornmeal. When snack time arrived, Mrs. Johnson plugged in her electric grill and gave each child a little wad of arepa dough. He or she rolled the wad into a ball, then flattened it like a tortilla. Mrs. Johnson fried the dough on the grill.

"*Gracias,*" Camila said, as she chewed on the arepa.

Just before school ended, Mrs. Johnson let the class go outside for a short recess. Camila seemed surprised to see the swings and the brightly colored playground sets. "Was your playground like this in Colombia?" Carol asked her.

"No," Camila answered. "Our school had a small playground with just one play area that could be used for football—wait, I think you call it soccer?"

The two girls began swinging, and Carol tried to think of what else to talk about. She played softball and had just started taking violin lessons, so she asked, "Do you play a musical instrument?"

"Yes," Camila said. "We take lots of music lessons in school. I played the drum in the school marching band. What kind of music do you like?"

"I play the violin, but I like to listen to Shakira," Carol said.

"Me too!" Camila said. "Did you know Shakira is from Colombia? Her song 'Hips Don't Lie' helped me learn English."

Shakira was born on February 2, 1977, in Baranquilla, a city on Colombia's Caribbean coast. From an early age, it was clear that Shakira was a performer. She studied acting, singing, and dancing, although she seemed to pick up belly dancing all on her own. In 2006 she reached worldwide fame with her hit song "Hips Don't Lie." Shakira's Bare Feet Foundation helps poor children in Colombia go to school.

Camila loved to watch the La Mesa parade every year. The parade is held to celebrate the founding of La Mesa on March 12, 1777.

Carol wondered if she and Camila would find more things they had in common. "My cousins are coming soon," she said. "Maybe we can all go sledding together."

"I would like that! I've never played in the snow," said Camila. "Only the highest mountains have snow in Colombia."

Now Carol really hoped it would snow so that she and her cousins could go sledding with her new friend.

Colombian peasants, or farmers, have traditionally decorated their homes with collages made from the beans and seeds that are readily available. Corn, coffee, rice, and beans are staples of the Colombian diet, so making art with them is also a way to acknowledge their importance to the culture.

Instructions for Making a Traditional Colombian Collage

1 On a piece of cardboard, draw a design. You can create a landscape, with a farmhouse and hills, or write something, such as *Bienvenido*, which means "welcome," or *Paz*, which means "peace."

2 Glue an assortment of beans, rice, corn, lentils, and coffee beans to the cardboard. The different beans and seeds will give your collage different colors and textures.

Further Reading

Books

Cameron, Sara. *Out of War: True Stories from the Front Lines of the Children's Movement for Peace in Colombia*. New York: Scholastic, 2001.

Morrison, Marion. *Colombia (Enchantment of the World)*. New York: Scholastic, 2007.

Murcia, Rebecca Thatcher. *Shakira*. Hockessin, Delaware: Mitchell Lane Publishers, 2007.

Streissguth, Thomas. *Colombia in Pictures*. Minneapolis: Lerner Publications Company, 2004

Colombian Tales

Brusca, Maria Cristina. *When Jaguars Ate the Moon and Other Stories about Animals and Plants of the Americas*. New York: Henry Holt, 1995.

Metaxes, Eric. *The Monkey People: A Colombian Folktale*. Edina, Minnesota: Abdo, 2005.

Magazine Articles

Anonymous. "Quake Shakes Colombia." *Scholastic News*, February 22, 1999, p. 3.

Murcia, Rebecca Thatcher. "A New World." *Scholastic News*, September 29, 2003, p. 4.

On the Internet

National Geographic's Colombia website
http://www3.nationalgeographic.com/places/countries/country_colombia.html

NOAA: Nevado del Ruiz Facts and Figures
http://www.ngdc.noaa.gov/hazard/stratoguide/nevadofact.html

Shakira's Bare Feet Foundation
http://www.fundacionpiesdescalzos.com/

Further Reading

Works Consulted
This book is based on author Rebecca Thatcher Murcia's personal experiences living in Colombia and being part of a Colombian family. The author also consulted with Colombian friends and relatives while writing this book. Works consulted are listed below.

Bushnell, David. *Una Nación a Pesar de Si Misma*. Bogotá: Planeta, 2007.

Chomsky, Aviva, Garry Leech, and Steve Striffler. *The People Behind Colombian Coal: Mining, Multinationals and Human Rights*. Bogotá: Casa Editorial Pisando Callos, 2007.

Green, W. John. "Guerrillas, Soldiers, Paramilitaries, Assassins, Narcos, and Gringos: The Unhappy Prospects for Peace and Democracy in Colombia." *Latin American Research Review*. Austin, University of Texas Press, 2005.

Griswold, Eliza. "Medellin's Mean Streets." *National Geographic*. March 2005, pp. 73–91.

Hagen, Jason. "New Colombia President Promises More War." *NACLA Report on the Americas*. New York. July/August 2002, pp. 24–29.

Library of Congress. *A Country Study: Colombia* http://memory.loc.gov/frd/cs/cotoc.html

Parsa, Tim. "Colombian Gold." *New York Times Magazine* (Style), Summer 2007, p. 122.

Schemo, Diana Jean. "Noisy Game In Colombia: Big Danger Is the Player." *New York Times*, December 26, 1997. http://query.nytimes.com/gst/fullpage.html?res=9501EFDA1E3EF 935A15751C1A961958260

Embassy
The Embassy of Colombia/*Embajada de Colombia*
2118 Leroy Place, NW
Washington, DC 20008
Phone: (202) 387-8338
Email: emwas@colombiaemb.org
http://www.colombiaemb.org/

PHOTO CREDITS: Cover, pp. 1, 2, 3, 18, 35—Jupiter images; p. 9, 16—AP Photo/Ricardo Mazalan; p. 15—AP Photo/Marcelo Hernandez; p. 12—Jonathan Scott; pp. 29, 30, 33, 39—Getty Images; p. 26—Barbara Marvis; pp. 32, 34, 40—Rebecca Thatcher Murcia; p. 48—Peggy Fogarty-Harnish

Glossary

assassinated (uh-SASS-ih-nay-ted)—Killed for political reasons.

atmosphere (AT-mus-feer)—The air around Earth.

canal (kah-NAL)—A waterway cut through land that allows boats to pass.

Chibchas (CHEEP-chas)—Members of one of the most important groups of native people in Colombia.

colonist (KAH-luh-nist)—A person who settles in a new land that is still governed by his or her original country.

conservation (kon-ser-VAY-shun)—The act of taking care of the environment.

cordillera (KOOR-dee-yer-uh)—The Spanish word for a mountain range.

democratic (deh-moh-KRAH-tik)—Ruled by the majority vote of the people.

dictator (DIK-tay-tur)—The head of a government in which one person holds power.

endangered (en-DAYN-jerd)—In trouble; at risk of dying out.

guerrilla (guh-RIH-luh)—A member of an independent army of soldiers that fights an established government.

independence (in-dee-PEN-dents)—Self-rule.

isthmus (IS-mus)—A narrow strip of land between bodies of water that connects larger areas of land.

Latin America (LAA-tin uh-MAYR-ih-kuh)—The parts of the Americas settled by the Spanish and now governed mainly by their descendants; includes most of South America, Central America, Mexico, Cuba, Puerto Rico, the Dominican Republic, and some of the islands in the West Indies.

peninsula (peh-NIN-suh-luh)—A strip of land that juts out into water.

revolutionaries (reh-vuh-LOO-shuh-nay-rees)—People who want to overthrow a government.

socialist (SOH-shuh-list)—The political belief that the government should control the economy so that citizens are treated more fairly.

tejo (TAY-hoh)—A popular Colombian game in which a small heavy disk is thrown at a target.

traffickers (TRAA-fih-kers)—People who move illegal goods from one country to another.

unified (YOO-nih-fyd)—Brought together under one government.

Index

ABOUT THE AUTHOR

Rebecca Thatcher Murcia is the author of many books for children, including *Shakira*, *Ronaldinho*, and *David Beckham* for Mitchell Lane Publishers. Her husband, Saúl Murcia, grew up in Colombia. After he died of cancer in 2005, Rebecca and her two sons, Gabriel and Mario, and their dog, Crystal, moved to La Mesa, a small town in Colombia. Gabriel and Mario enrolled in school in La Mesa, and also played for the town's soccer and tennis teams. During their time off from school, they explored Colombia's Caribbean coast, snorkeling in Las Islas Rosarios and playing in the waves in Cartagena.